This content of this book may be used by all people of good will as we humans collectively seek to create a loving, sustainable and harmonious Earth.

Composed by Richard Arnold
Brunswick, Victoria, Australia
Designed by Theo Arnold
November 2024

The front cover and back cover image was produced by NASA and the Space Telescope Science Institute
(STSCI) from Nasa's James Webb Space Telescope.

The illustrations were made with generative AI images.

ISBN 978-0-6451296-3-2

Introduction

This thanksgiving greeting to the Universe has been inspired by the Thanksgiving Address to the Natural World of the Haudenosaunee people of North America.[1] It also incorporates an understanding of the journey of the Universe in the light of modern scientific knowledge. It gives thanks for the whole of creation from its primal beginnings.

This latter "big picture" context has been inspired by recent theologians such as Thomas Berry[2] who talks the need for a "New Story" to help guide humanity into a sustainable future. The underlying message of the New Story is that the Universe has been evolving from the very beginning. This project of Loving Source burst forth from its own overflowing love and all beings are invited to be part of the evolving journey in their own unique way.

For human beings this particularly involves discerning how their unique gifts given by the divine energy of the Universe, might be used to engage with the evolutionary unfolding of creation itself as the Universe continues its incredible journey toward fulfilment.

---

[1] *Thanksgiving Address: Greetings to the Natural World English version: John Stokes and Kanawahienton (David Benedict, Turtle Clan/Mohawk) Mohawk version: Rokwaho (Dan Thompson, Wolf Clan/Mohawk) Original inspiration: Tekaronianekon (Jake Swamp, Wolf Clan/Mohawk)*

[2] *Berry, Thomas Mary, The Great Work, Three Rivers Press, New York, 1999*

In a world of frenetic activity and diverse voices, it is easy to become distracted from the divine energy of the Universe given by Loving Source. This greeting can be used each morning to help reconnect, re-centre and discern our way forward as participants in the Project of Loving Source.

The Greeting

We gather today as people of the Universe, living on the place we call Earth. There are many things for which we would like to give thanks.

The Project of our Loving Source

We give thanks that our Loving Source began a Project which arose out of overflowing love, with divine energy pulsing through the Universe, revealing the innate nature of Loving Source – relationship, being present for the other, and inter-dependency.

The divine energy continues to empower an evolving Universe, in which all beings are invited to participate.

The Heavens

We give thanks to the Sun which continues to bathe us in life-living energy, and to the planets, the moon, the stars and galaxies.

Mother Earth and the Natural World

We are thankful that the Universe has created our beautiful Mother Earth who teaches us, sustains us, and cares for us. We give thanks to the natural world – waters, soil, air, wind, rain, and all living things; trees, plants, insects, birds, fish, and animals. We give thanks to the rivers, lakes, mountains and plains.

Food, Plants and Creatures

We give thanks to the plants and creatures who offer themselves for our survival.
For many generations, they have given us fruits, seeds, grains, nuts, vegetables, dairy, eggs, and all other types of food.

The Waters and the Air

We give thanks to the waters of many kinds; rain and mist, river, lakes, seas. They give life by enabling plants and creatures to grow and thrive. The air breathes life into all creatures.

The Human Family

We give thanks to the Universe that it has created humans. We give thanks for the richness and diversity of the human family. As humans we have absorbed 13.7 billion years of creativity – we are the Universe in human form, able to celebrate the incredible journey.

The Courage To Be

We give thanks to guides such as Jesus who embodied the nature of Loving Source in his human life.

Jesus showed that pain, rejection, uncertainty, failure and death are not a barrier to the Universe reaching its fulfilment.

The spirit of Jesus enables humans to discover the courage to be and to "give life a go". We can accept the invitation to become partners in the love inspired Project of Loving Source. We can trust the Universe and strive to live in a mutually enhancing way.

The Gifts Of The Universe

We give thanks that the Universe shapes us through Mother Earth and gives all beings gifts which can be given back in unique ways in response to the invitation to become co-creators, each playing a unique part in shaping the future in a mutually enhancing way.

Deep Belonging

We give thanks that we and all beings have evolved together with the unfolding of the Universe in a mutually enhancing way. Each unique contribution and passion for life becomes imprinted on the Universe for eternity. In this way, all beings belong to the Universe in both Earthly time and after Earthly time.

Hope For The Future

Our motivation to "give life a go" is grounded in the Easter Mystery – new connected life emerges despite the deepest separation through embracing the spirit of Jesus. We can be confident that Loving Source's love inspired Project is still unfolding, and that Mother Earth and the Universe will continue to be renewed and fulfilled.

Spiritual Gifts

We give thanks for spiritual gifts which provide ways to continually reconnect – silence and stillness, rituals, music, communion and other creative expressions.

We give thanks for the gift of contemplation through which we can become free from the need to control and possess. In this way we experience a "luminous vastness" and deep relationship with the whole evolving journey of the Universe, and the freedom to live fully in each present moment.

The Peace

Now that we have given our thanks we are once again connected with ourselves, with each other and with all creation – we are community. We go in peace to be the Universe this day.

www.ingramcontent.com/pod-product-compliance
Lightning Source LLC
Chambersburg PA
CBRC090058010526
44109CB00039B/182